BREAKFASTGROUP

**Virtually in Alameda
K Gallery
at
Rhythmix Cultural Works**

September 12 – October 30, 2020

9781716699290

The Breakfast Group:
Virtually in Alameda

The Breakfast Group, a cohort of Berkeley artists who have been meeting weekly for decades, is delighted to convene digitally at the K Gallery at Rhythmix Cultural Works for a virtual exhibition!

Planned as an exhibition of painting, sculpture, and photography, the work has now shifted to the luminous plane of pixels. This is a group of artists who have been working in their studios, teaching in classrooms, curating in local institutions and then joining every week for discussions of exhibitions they have seen, books they have read, and films they have viewed. They mix the topical of sports with the immediacy of politics and circle back to the ever-present machinations of the art world – all with a hot cup of coffee in hand.

Back in the 1960s when a small group of artists –Elmer Bischoff, Erle Loran, and Sidney Gordon – started meeting once a week, they found camaraderie and mutual support in the free-ranging topics at the breakfast table. Over the years many friends were invited to join in the coffee fueled gatherings. Some people moved away, some returned, and some have passed on. But the spirit and soul of the group has continued now for over fifty years. Just as this movable feast of coffee and controversy, eggs and enthusiasms, toast and the topical has shifted venues and voices, today's members are facing profound change.

During this Novel Coronavirus Pandemic, requiring physical sheltering-in-place and a demanding degree of isolation, the Breakfast Group's weekly meal has been halted. But within that enormous void, we are replenished by this opportunity to share our artwork – paintings, sculpture, and photography – here in print and through the ether in an online exhibition presented by K Gallery at Rhythmix Cultural Works.

Breakfast for now may be alone at the kitchen table, but the mutual concern and support crosses the divide to merge vision and voice for an exhibition that addresses a broad spectrum of visual exploration. The Breakfast Group may only be virtually in Alameda, but the opportunity to examine the work for concerns of the environment, mortality, and beauty, this remains tangible.

– Jan Wurm

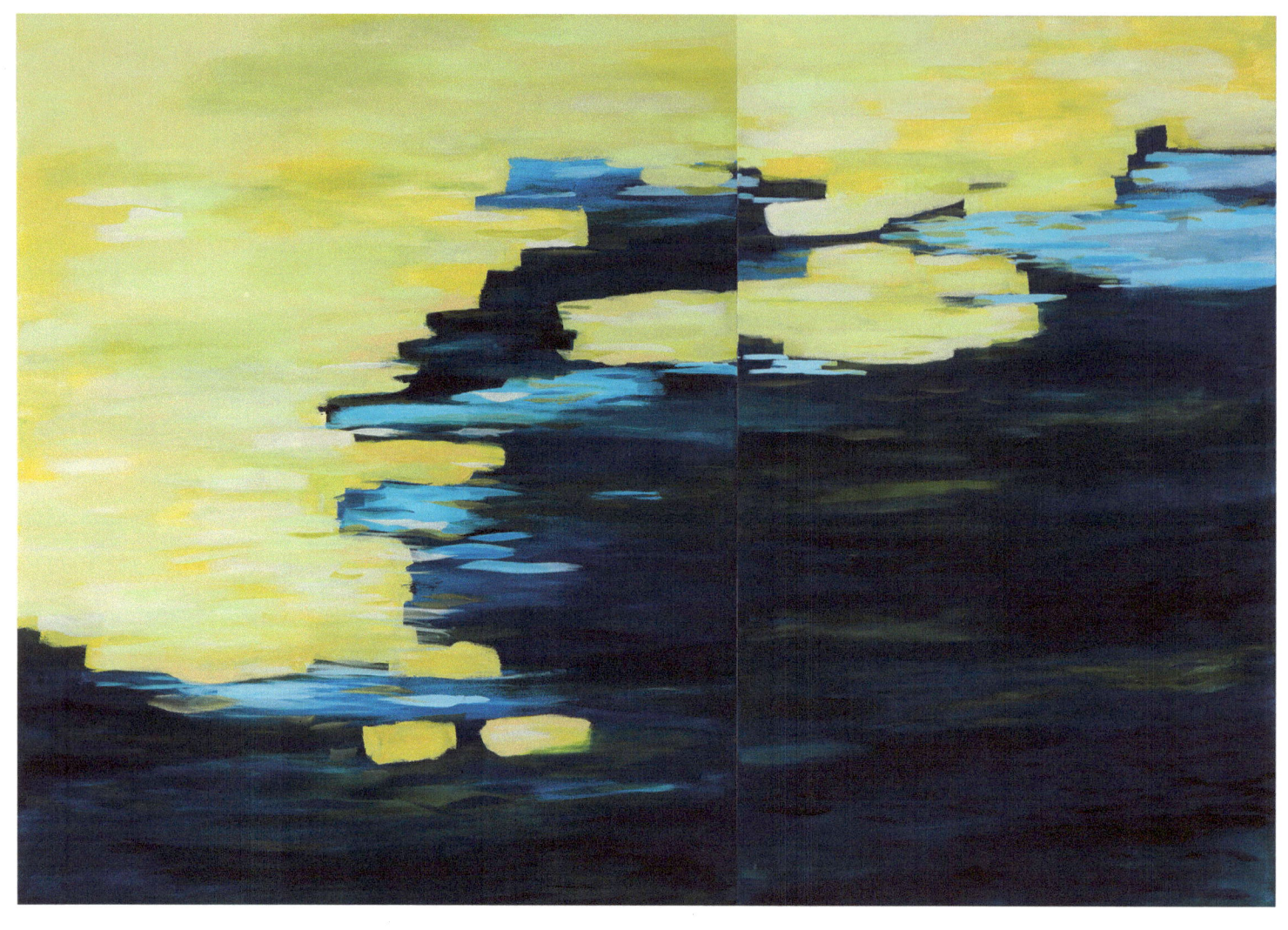

Donna Fenstermaker, *MVC Summer Pond 2,* 2020. Oil on canvas, 60x88 in.

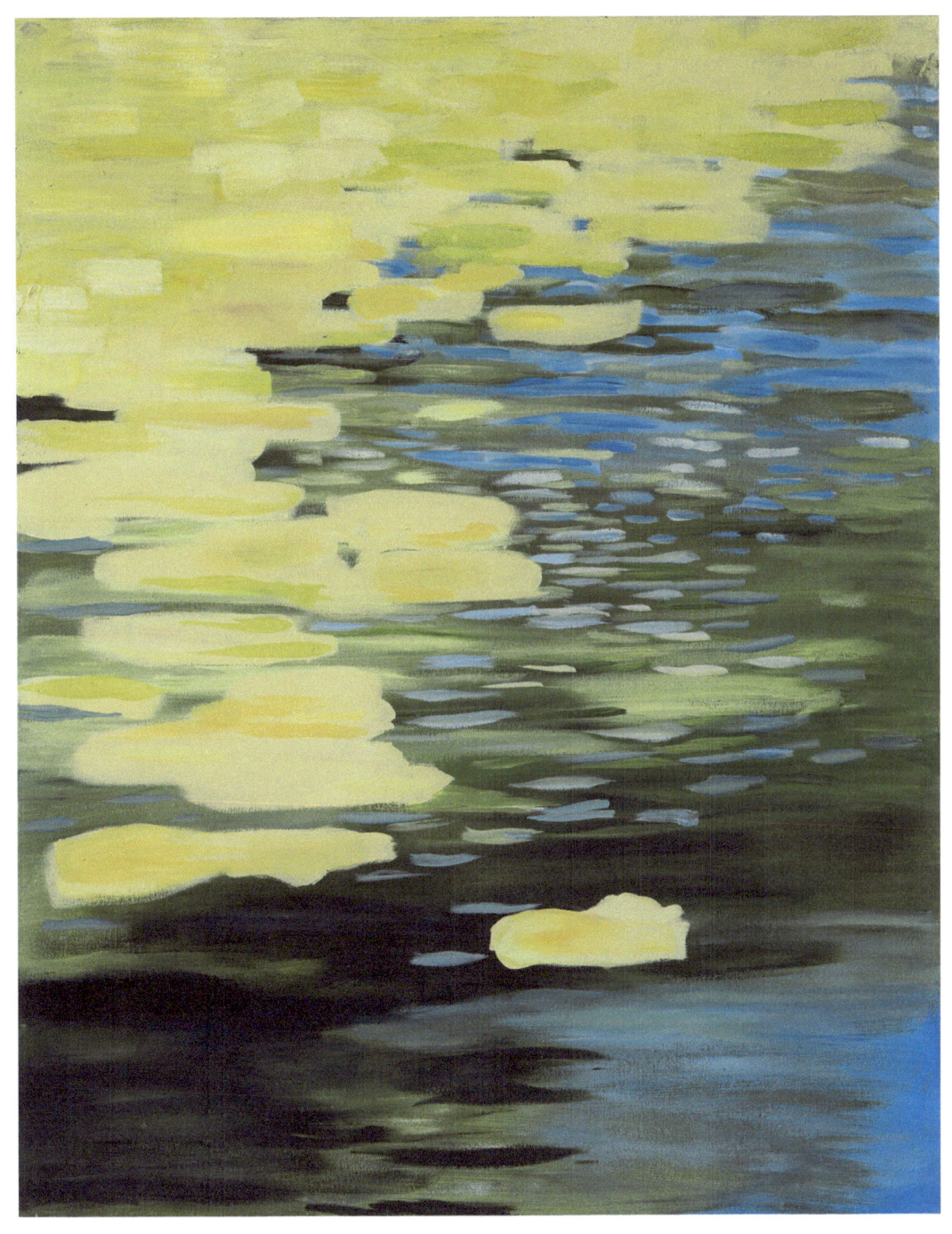

Donna Fenstermaker, *MVC Summer Pond 6.19*, 2019, Oil on canvas 55x40 in.

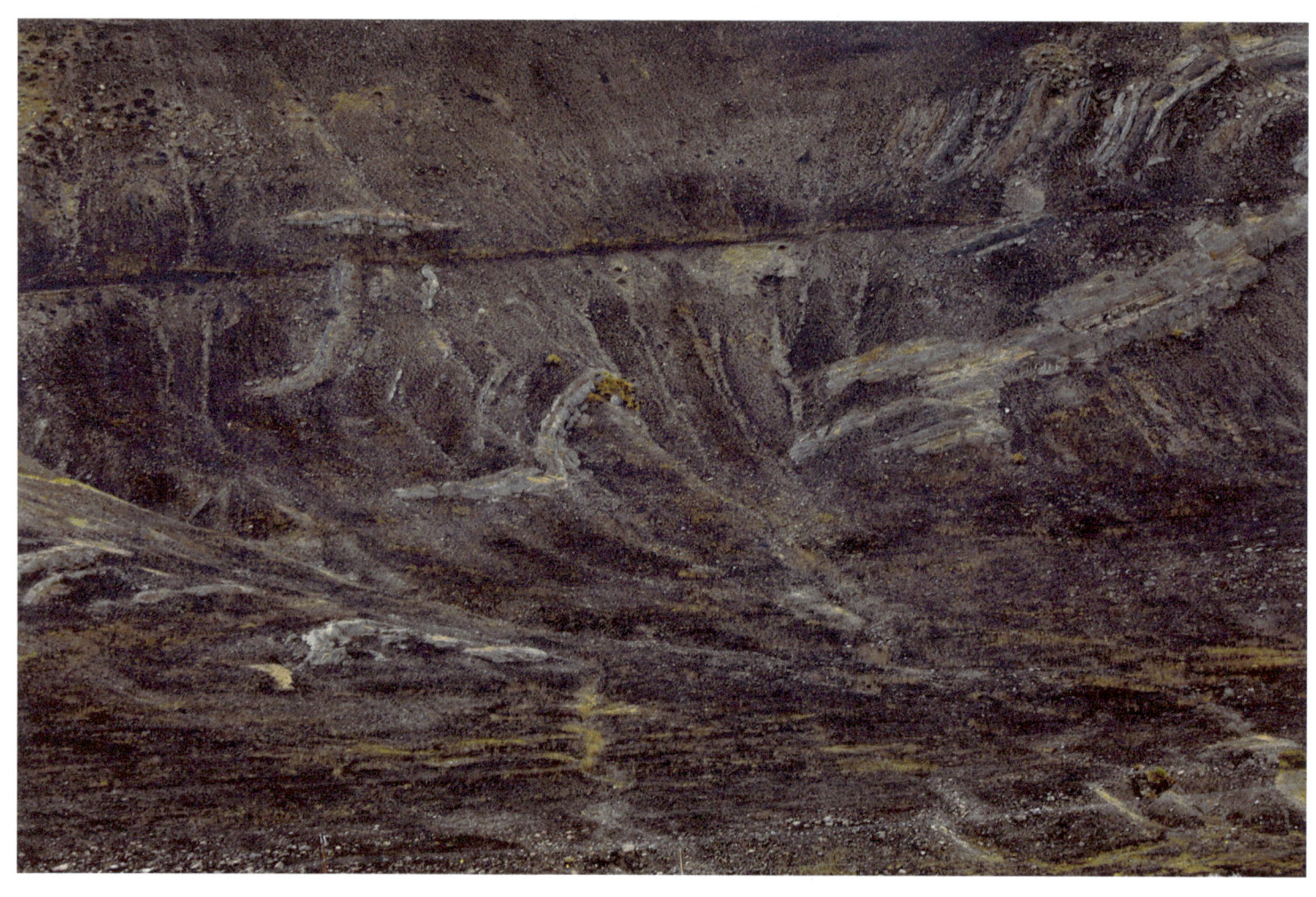

John Friedman, *US 6-191 Near Soldier Summit, UT*, 2019, Archival digital print, 22x20 in.

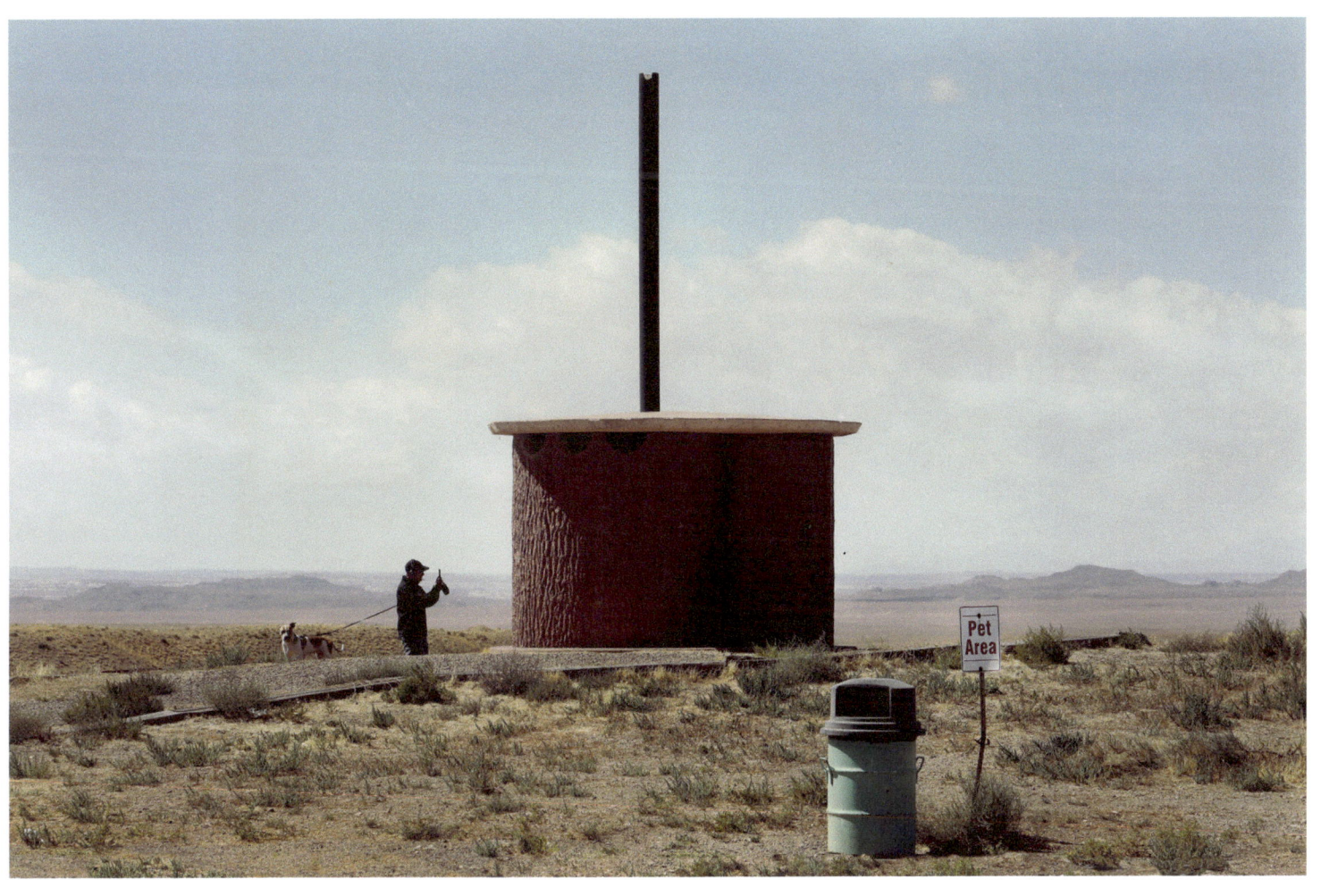

John Friedman, *Man and Nature near Thopmson Springs, September,* 2019, Archival digital print, 22x28in.

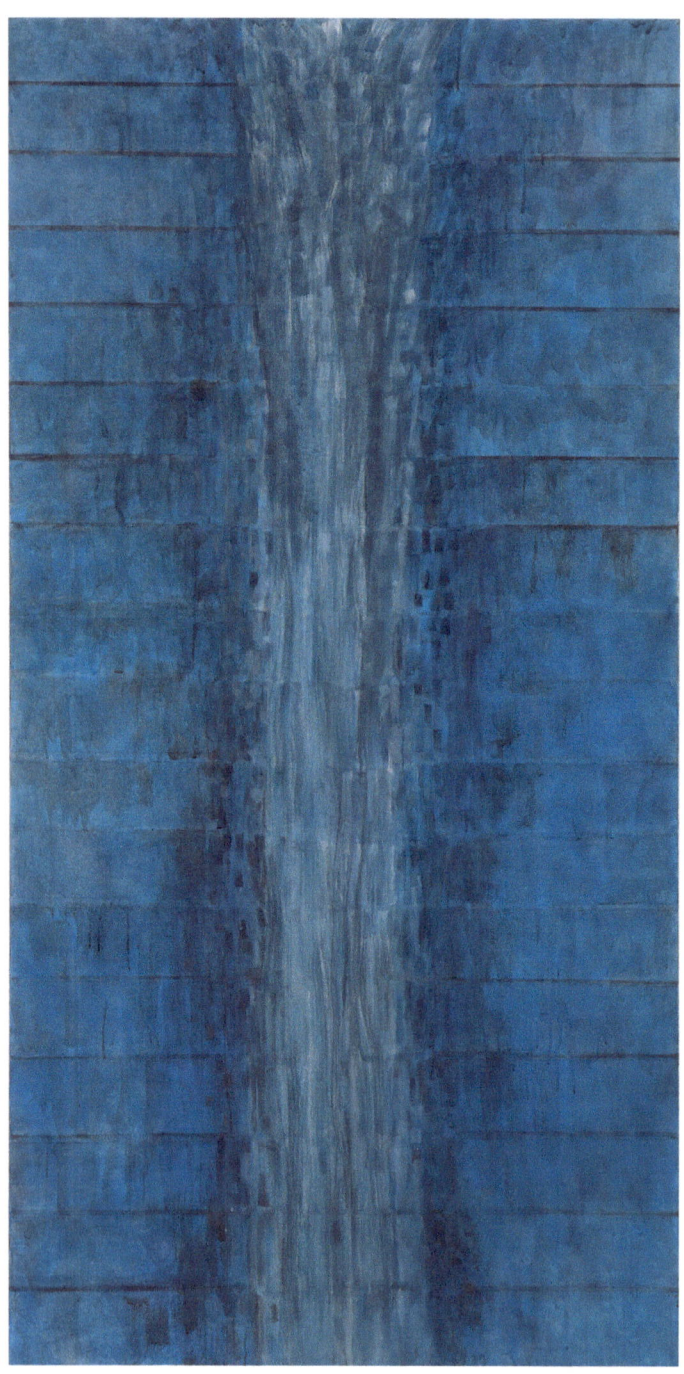

Nancy Genn, *Patagonia 39*, 2020, Casein on canvas, 72x36 in.

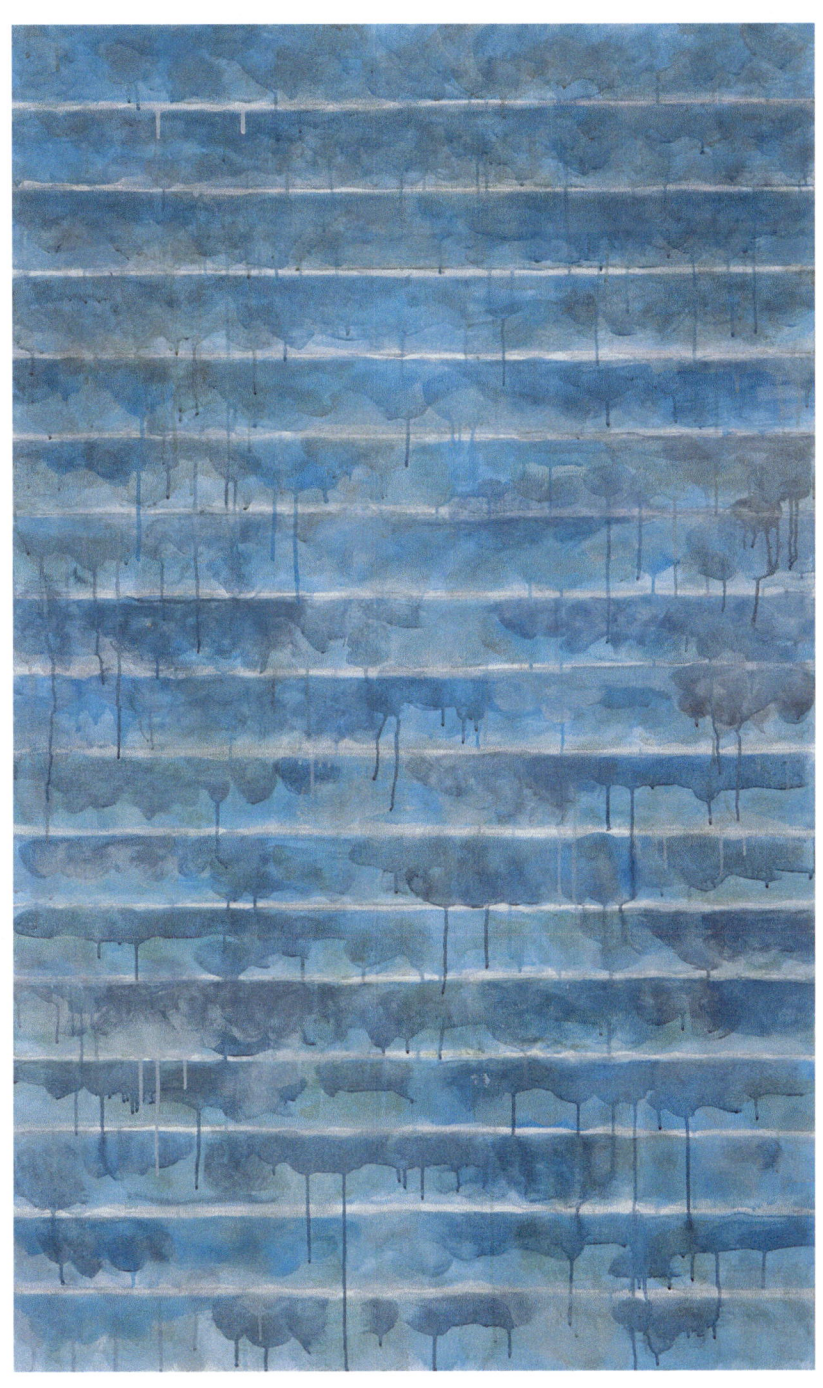

Nancy Genn, *Rainbars 25*, 2019, Casein on canvas, 60x36 in.

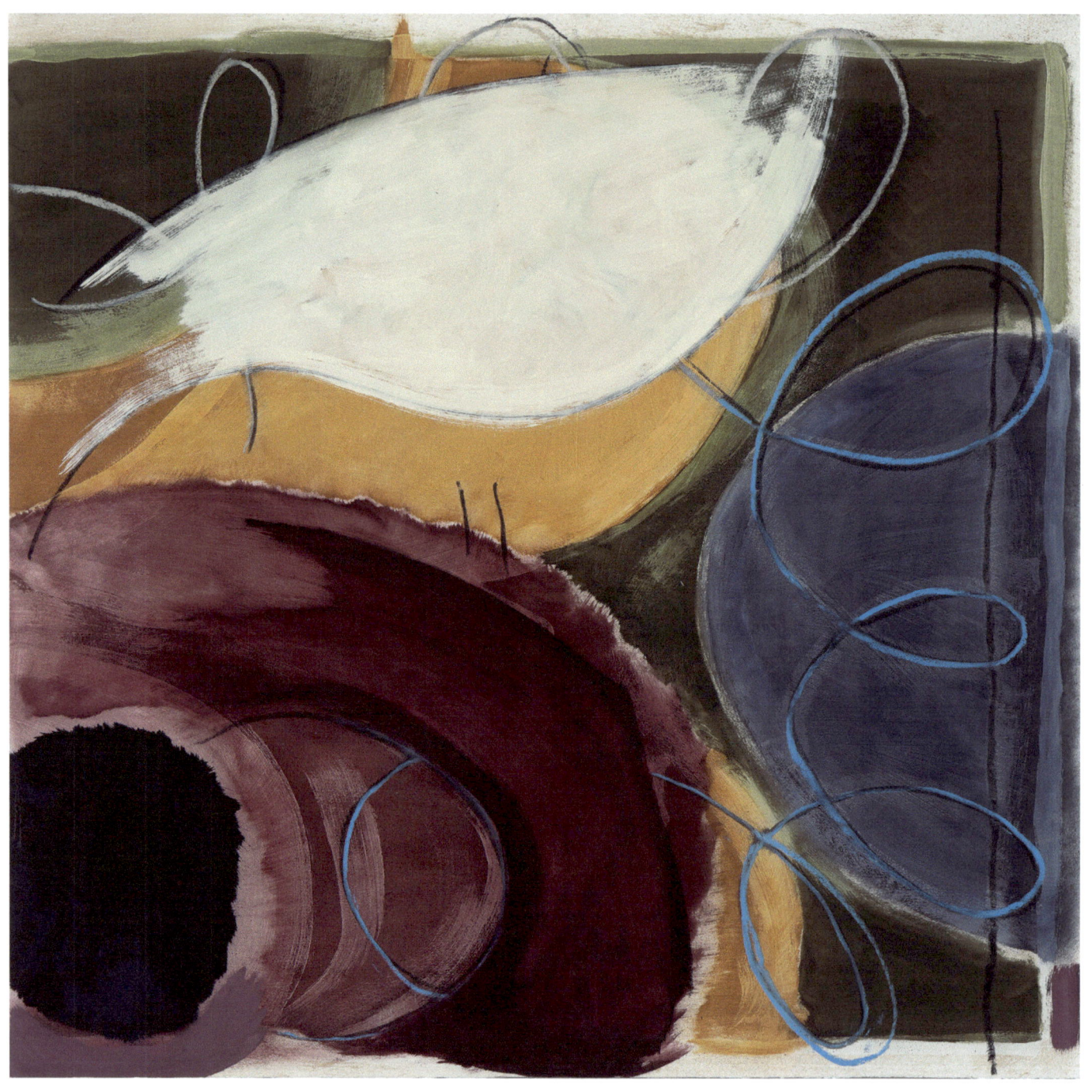

Katie Hawkinson, *Listening*, 2018, Oil on paper, 51x51 in.

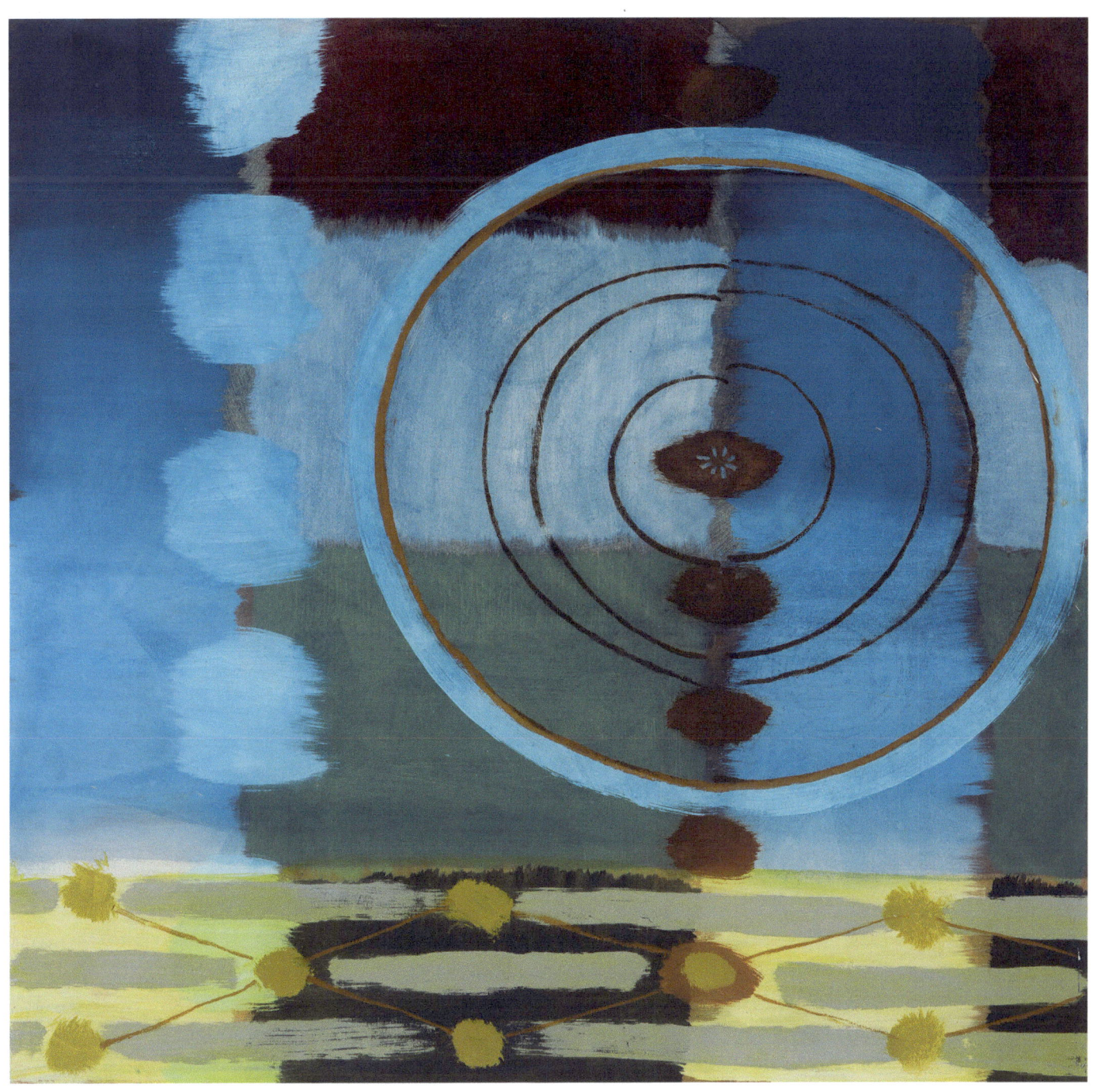

Katie Hawkinson, *Zephyr,* 2019, Oil on paper, 51x51 in.

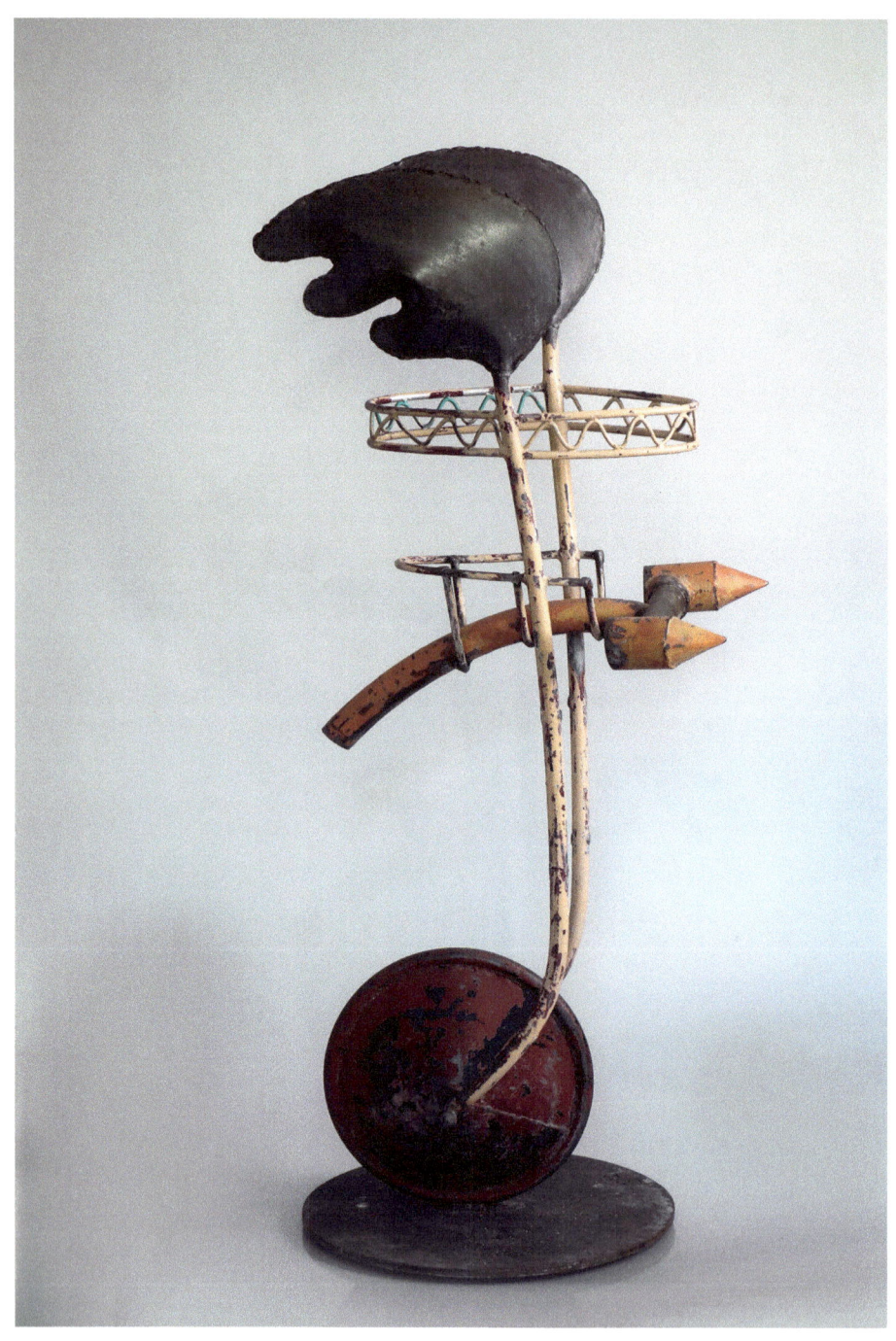

Stan Huncilman, *Etruscan Swan Song*, 2018, Sculpture welded and painted steel, 50x23x17 in.

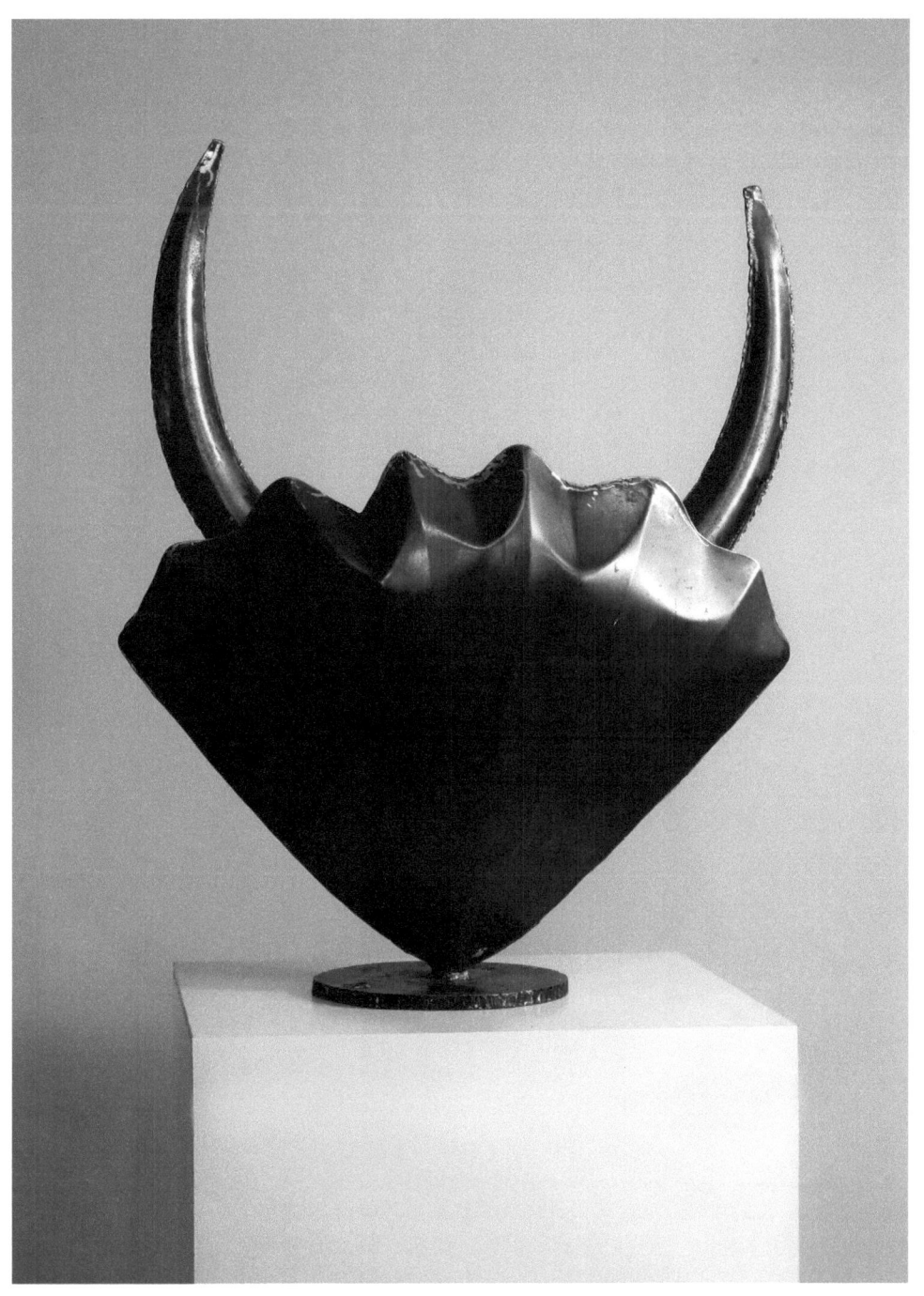

Stan Huncilman, *Rakes Homecoming*. 2018, Sculpture welded steel, 36x30x15 in.

Carol Ladewig, *Berkshire Fall*, 2019, Acrylic on canvas, 52x40x1.5 in.

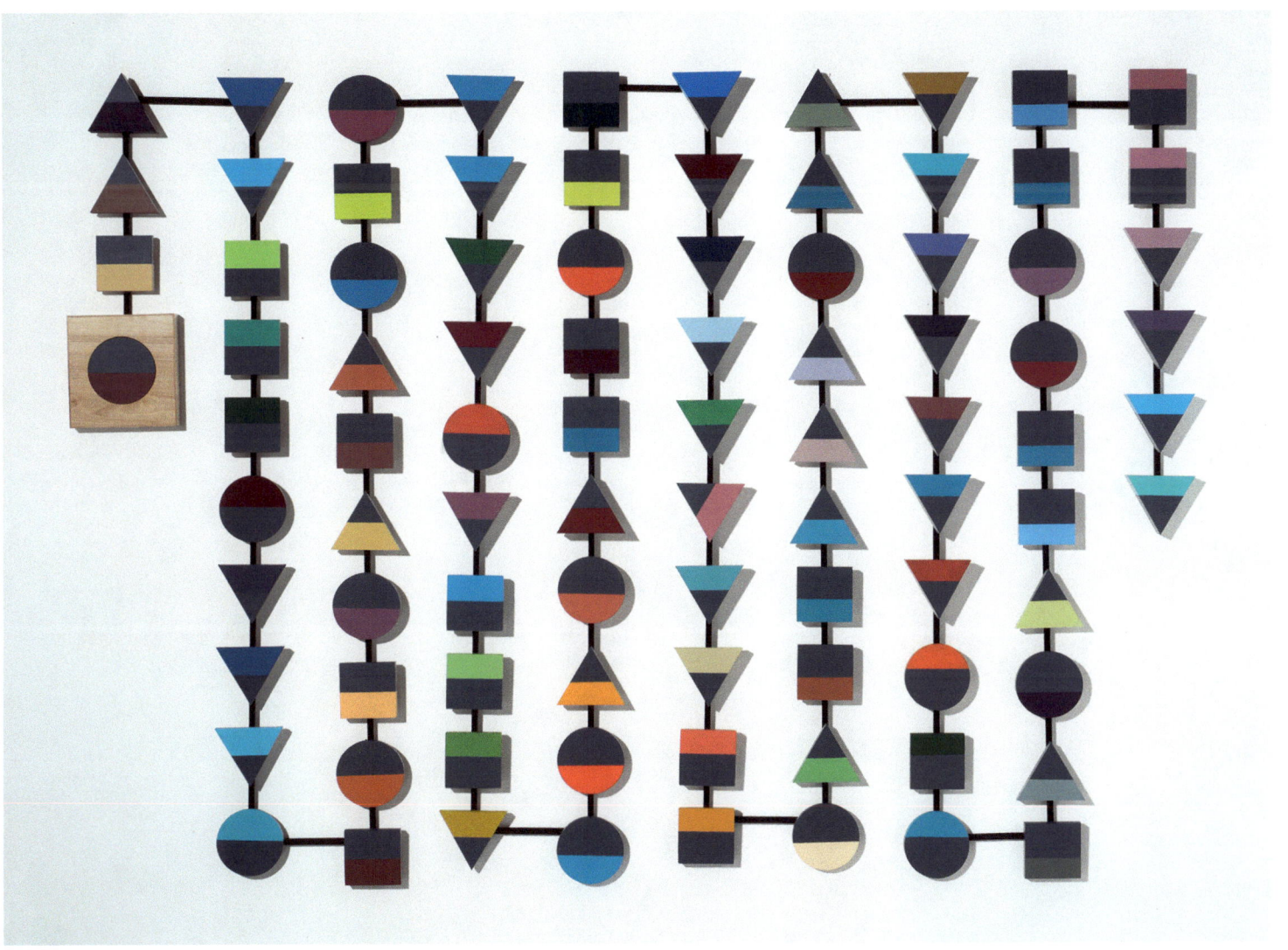

Carol Ladewig, *Fall 2018*, 2018, Acrylic gouache on wood panels, 70x135x2.5 in.

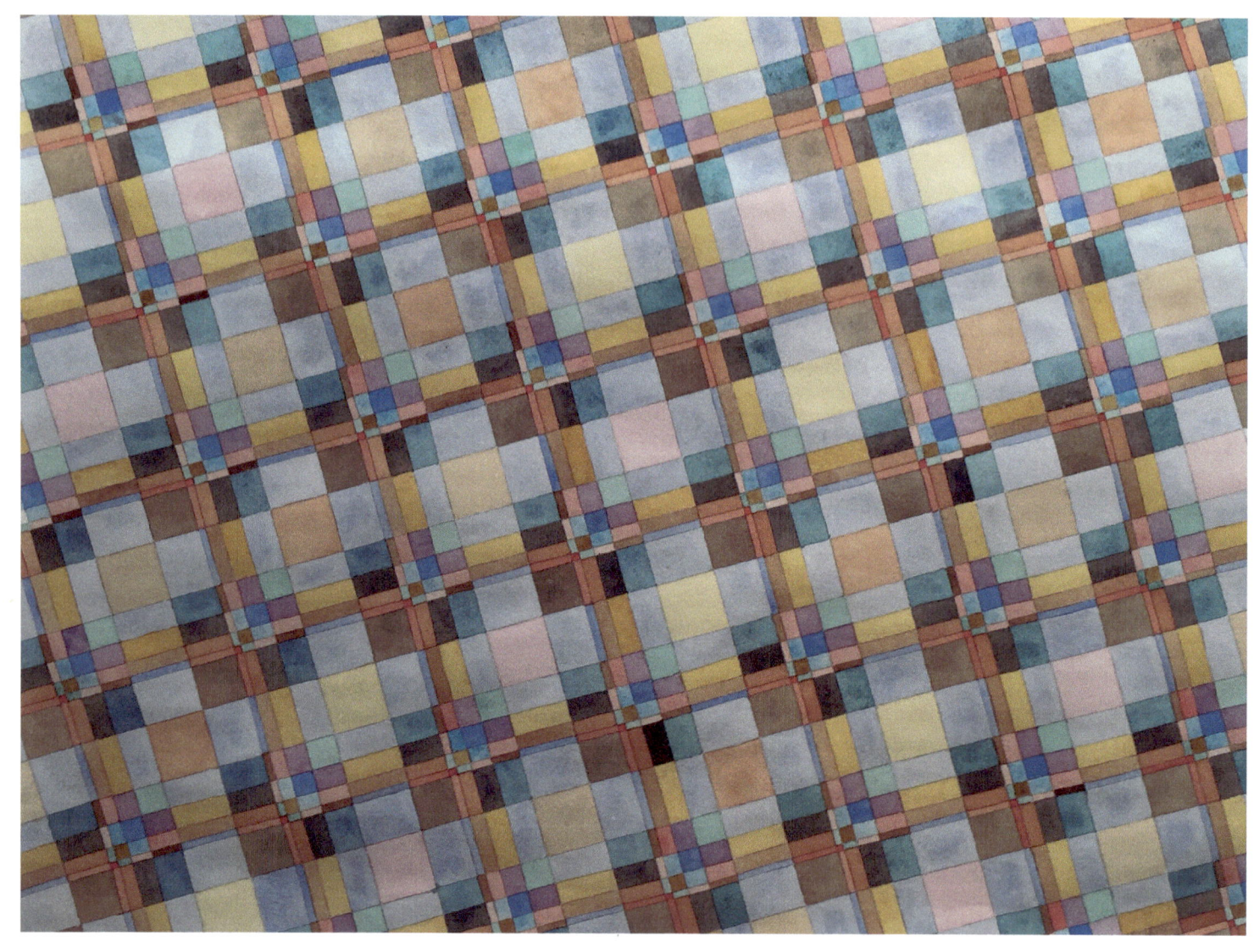

Loren Rehbock, *Plaid*, 2020, Watercolor on paper, 18x24 in.

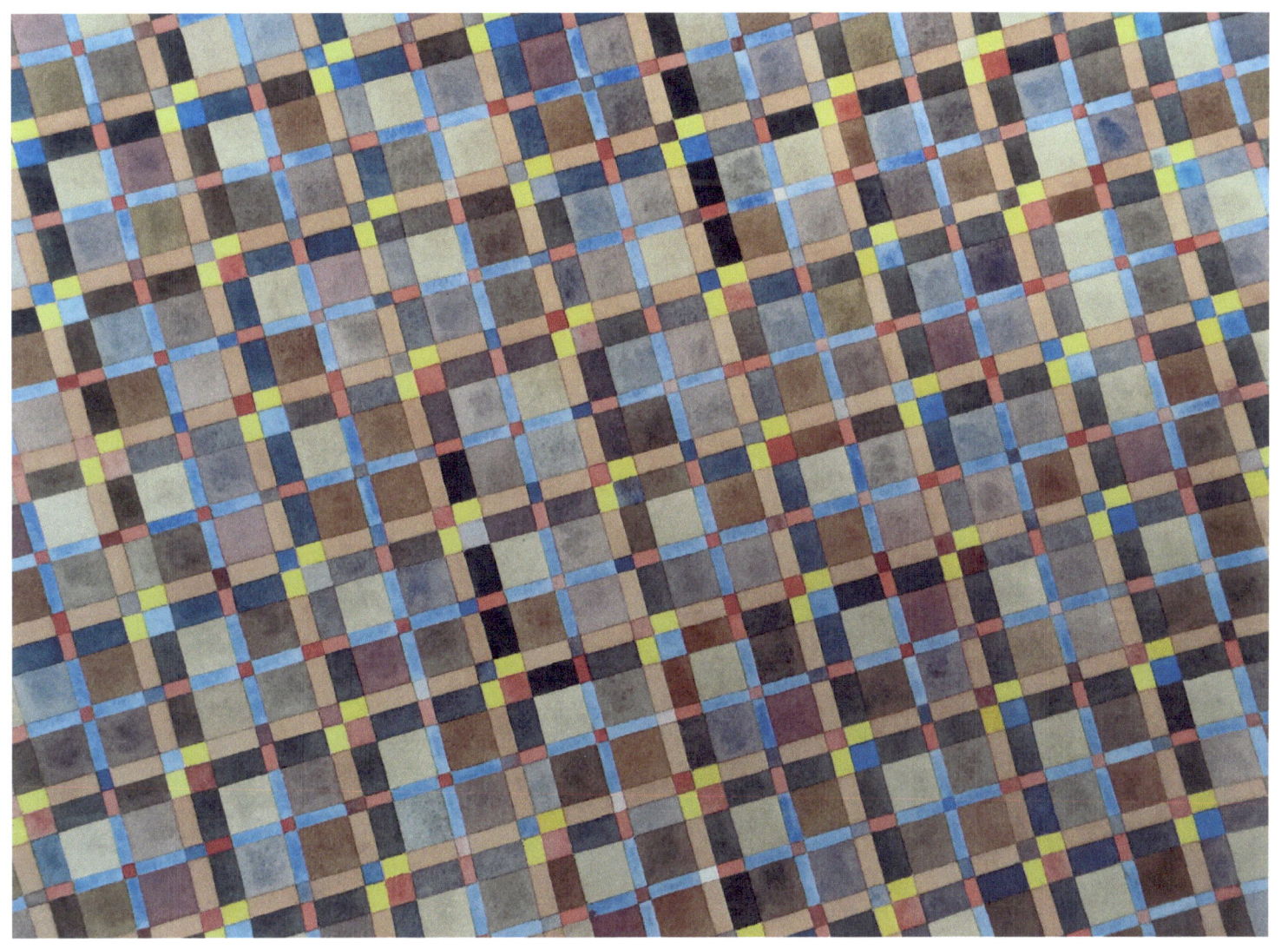

Loren Rehbock, *Plaid 2,* 2020, Watercolor on paper, 18x24 in.

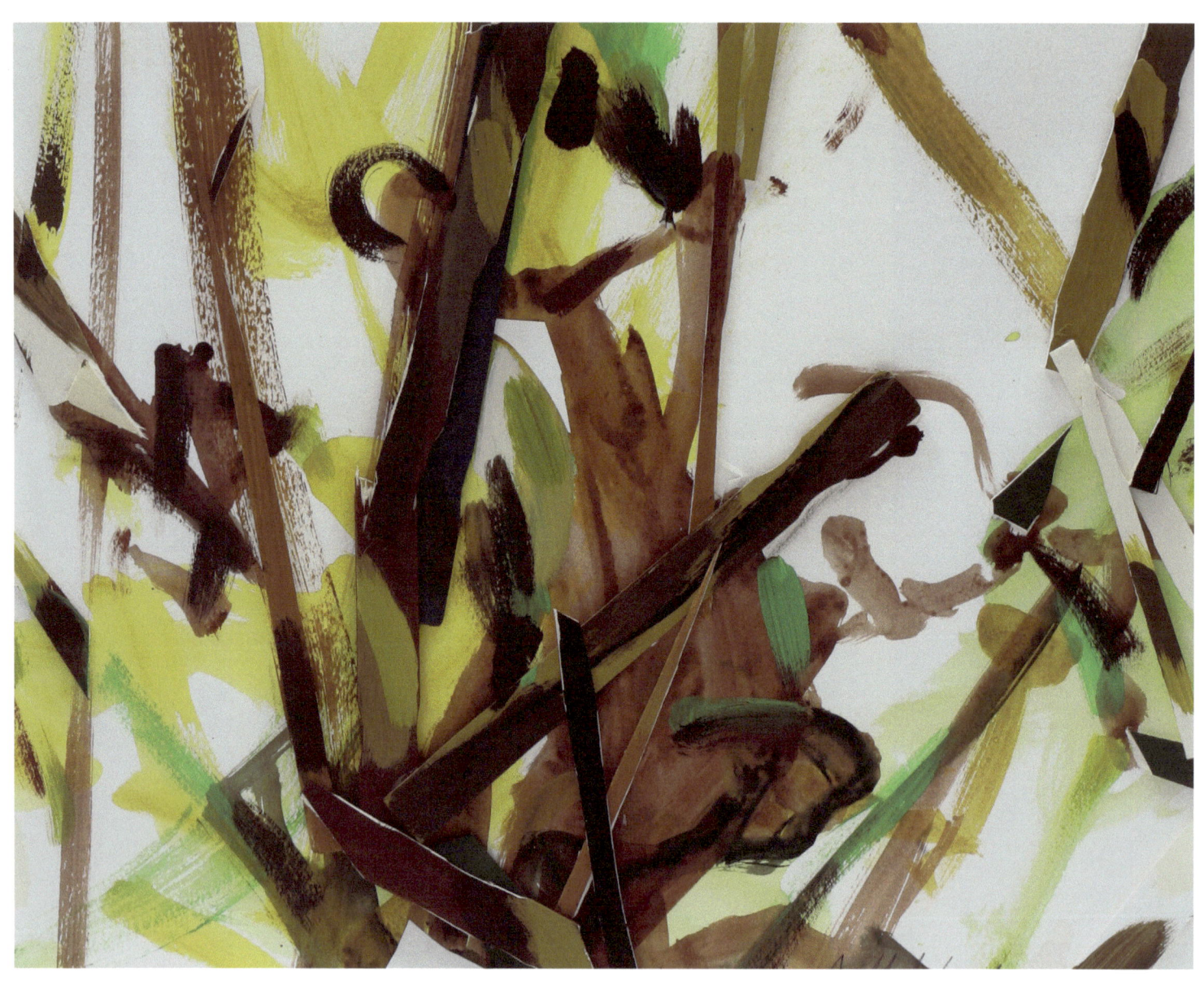

Foad Satterfield, *Hollis Street Parc #5*, n.d., Paper, acrylic, paint stick, on paper, 30x40 in.

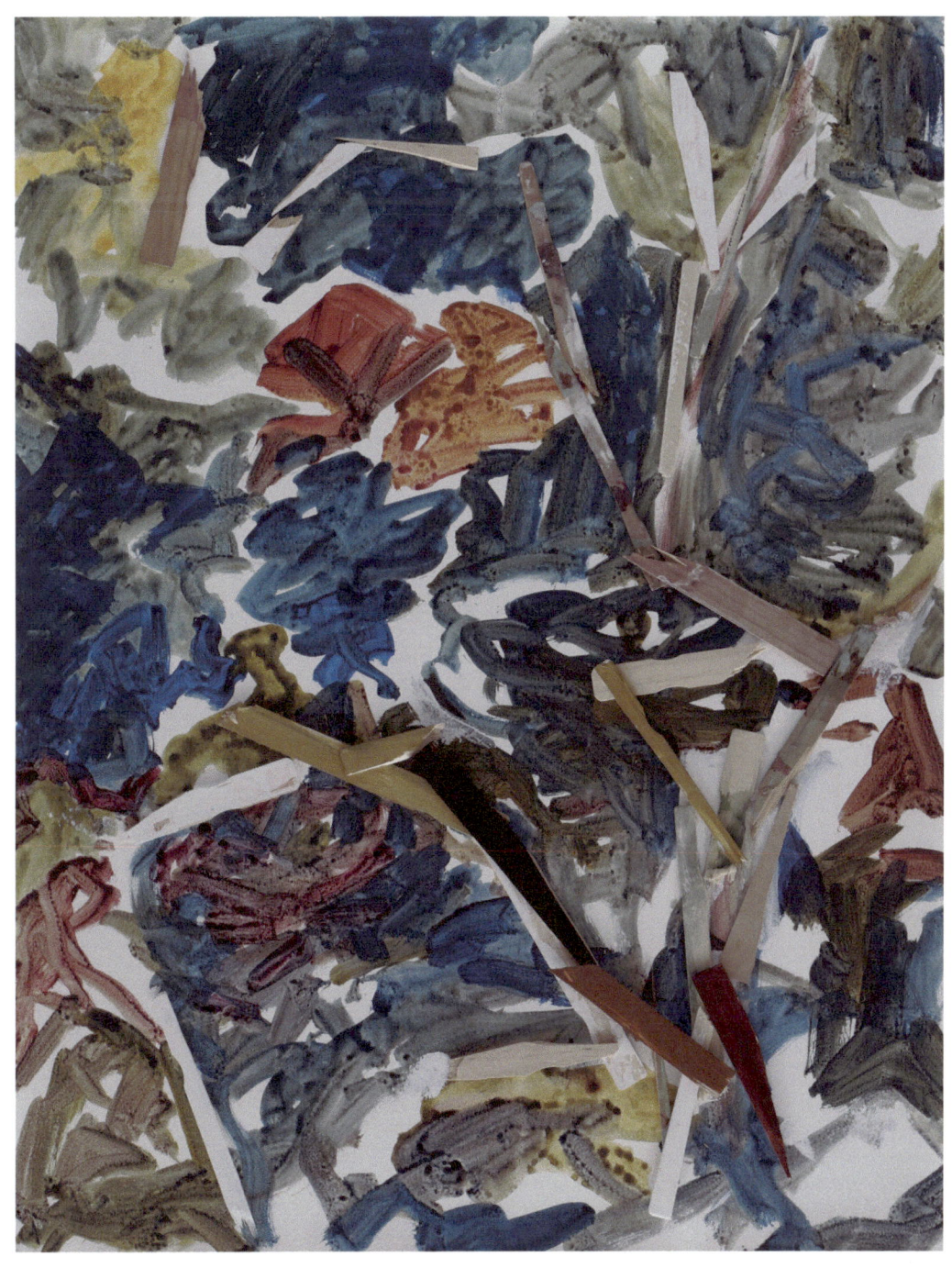

Foad Satterfield, *Hollis St #13*, n.d., Paper, acrylic, paint stick, on paper, 30x40 in. Collection Oumar Kiende

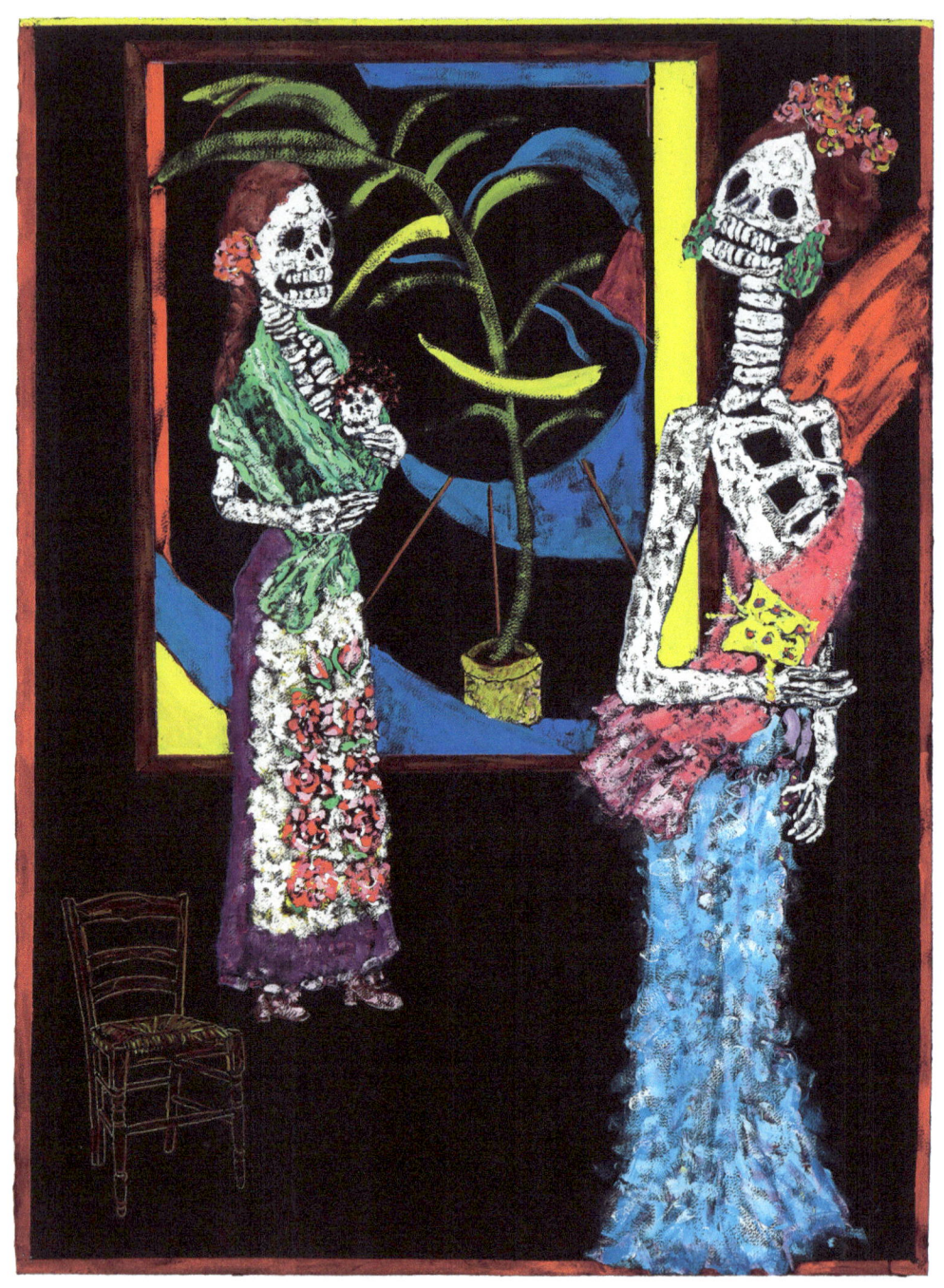

Robert Simons, *El Matrimonia #8Butterfly Bracelet 1*, 2014, acrylic, Gouache and pencil on paper, 44x30 in.

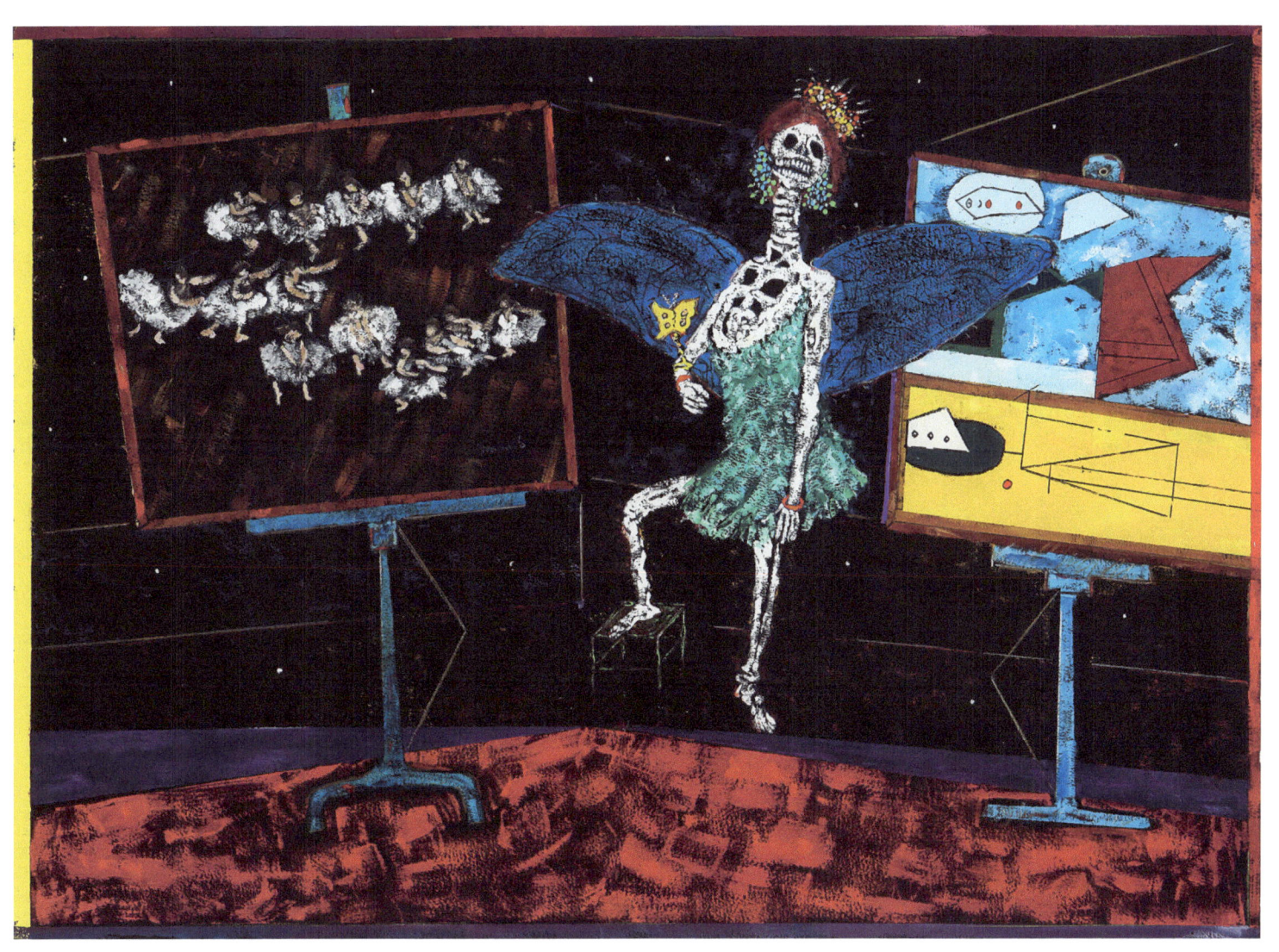

Robert Simons, *El Matrimonia #5 Butterfly Bracelet 2*, 2016, Gouache and pencil on paper, 22x30 in.

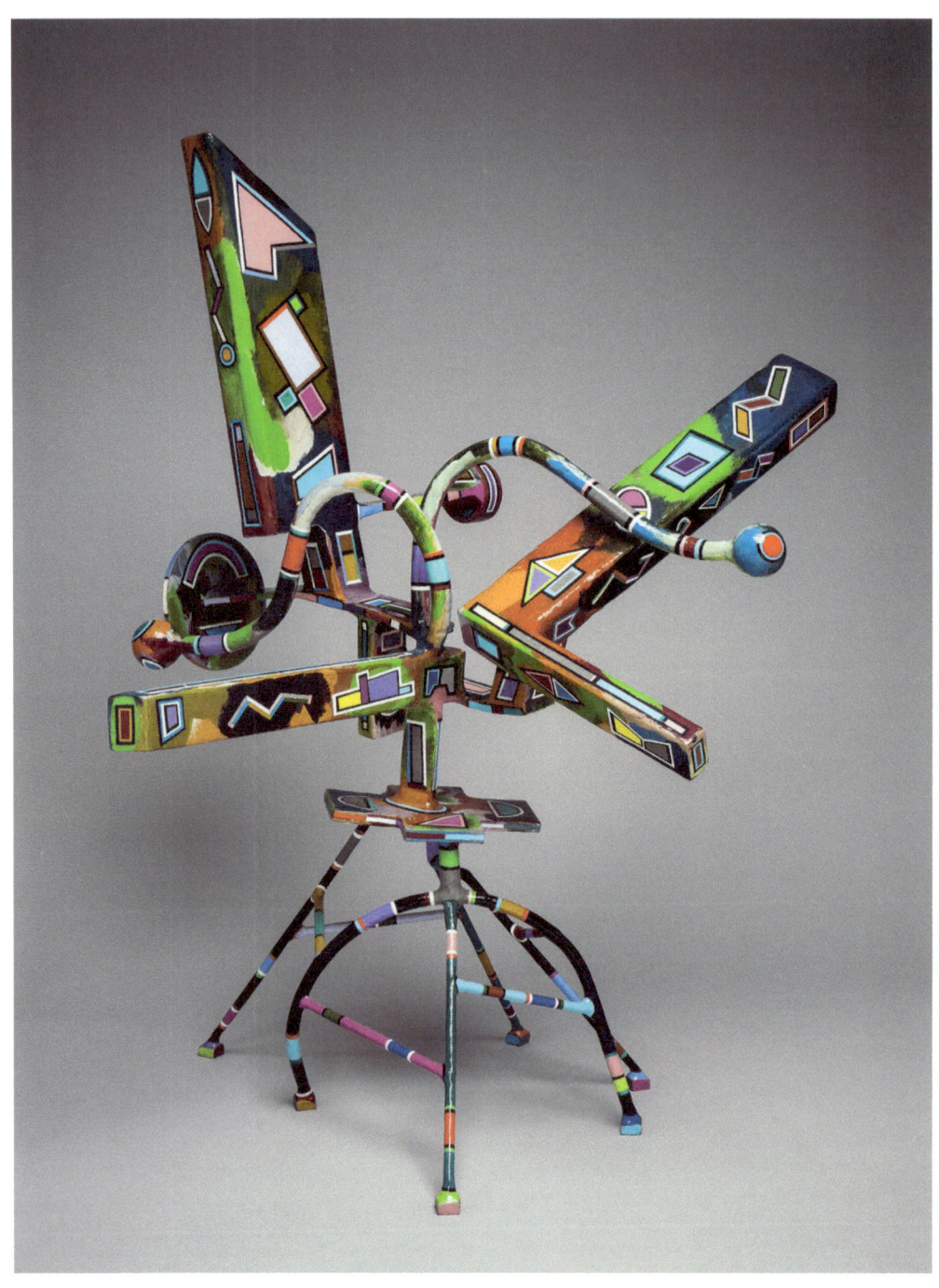

Joseph Slusky, *Obzor* 2012, Steel and acrylic laquer paint, 38x31x28 in.

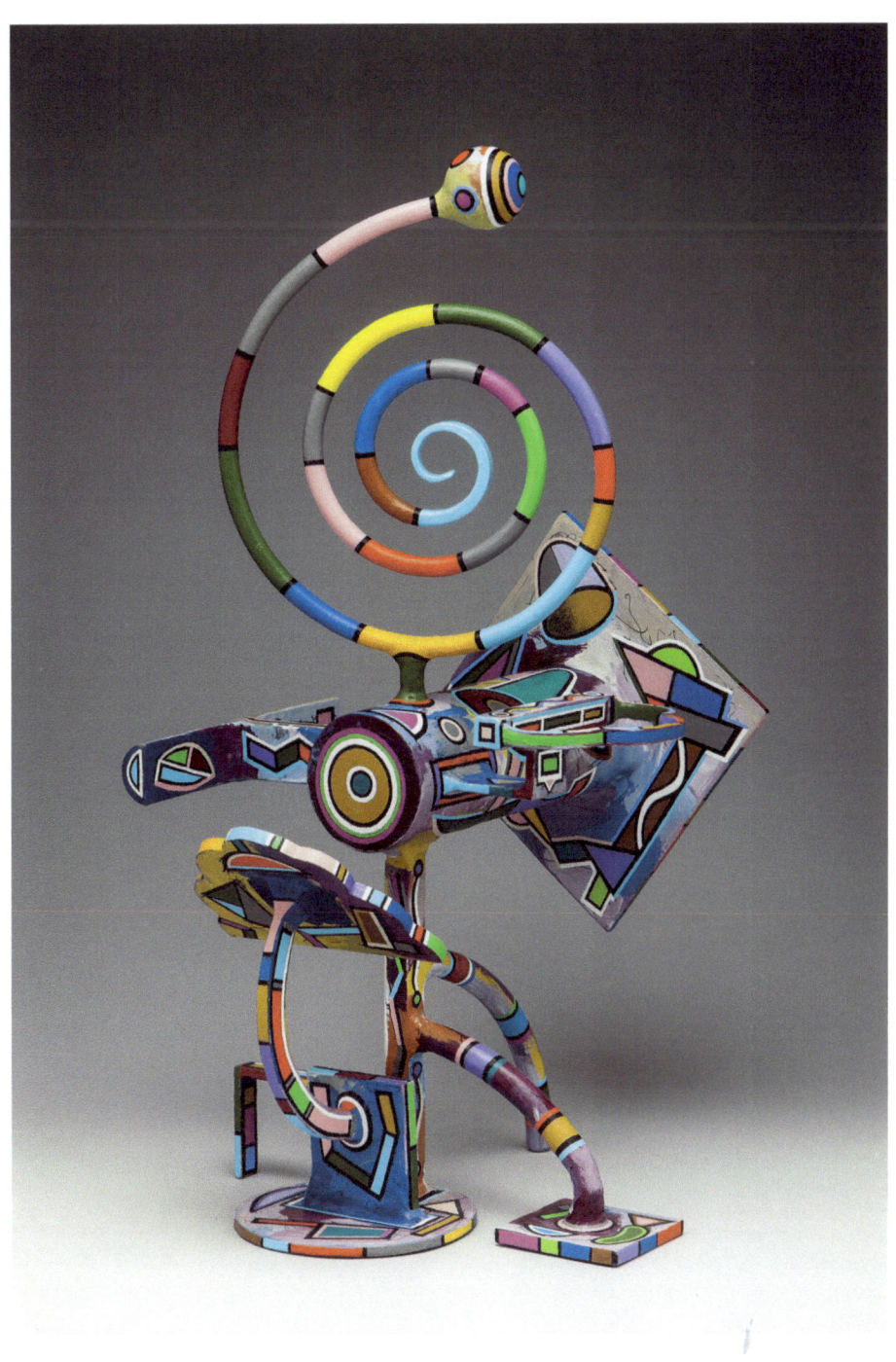

Joseph Slusky, *Shiloh*, 2017, Steel and acrylic laquer paint, 27x15x14 in.

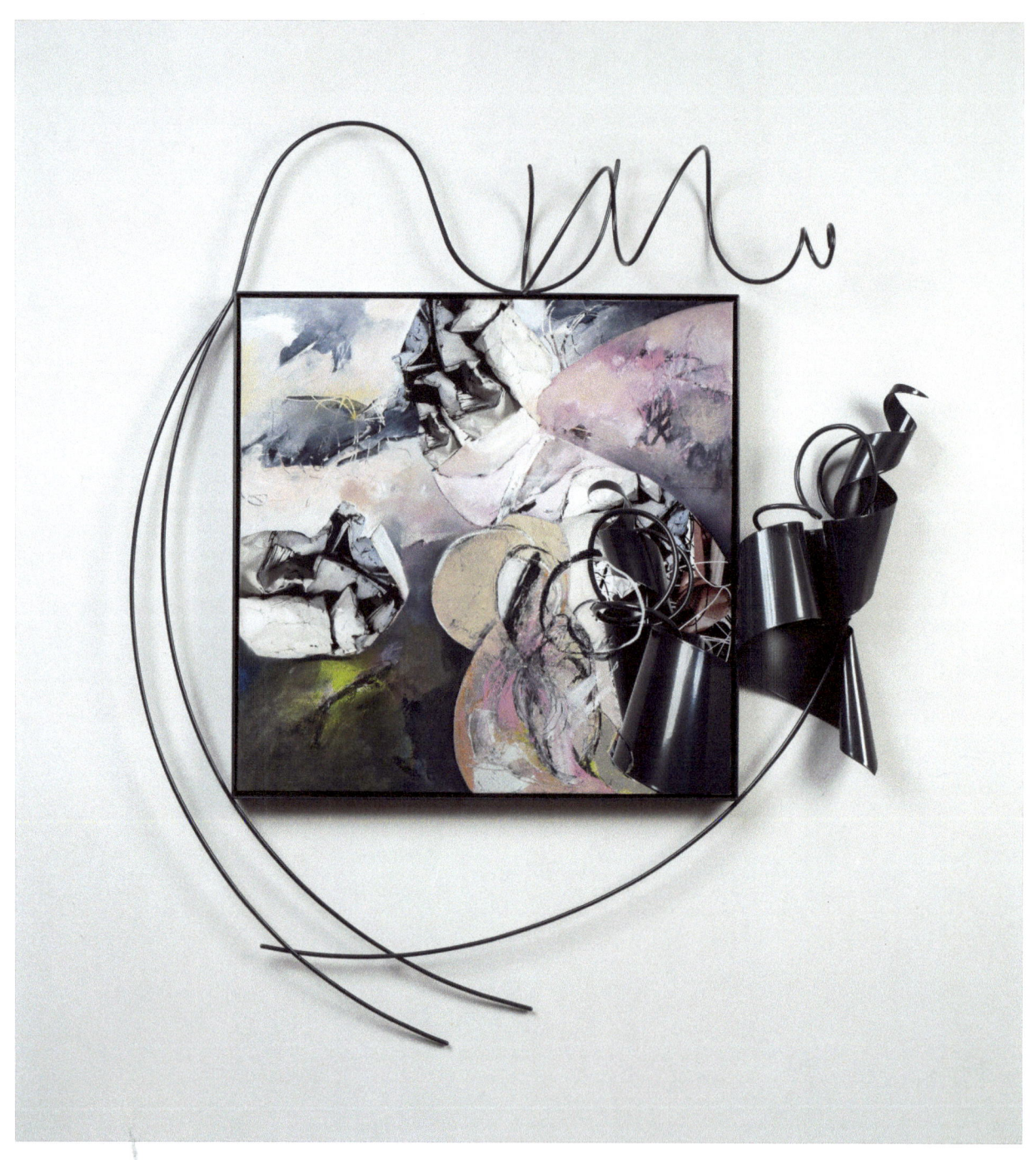

Kim Thoman, *Entanglement 9*, 2017, Oil and steel wall hanging, 60x55x10 in.

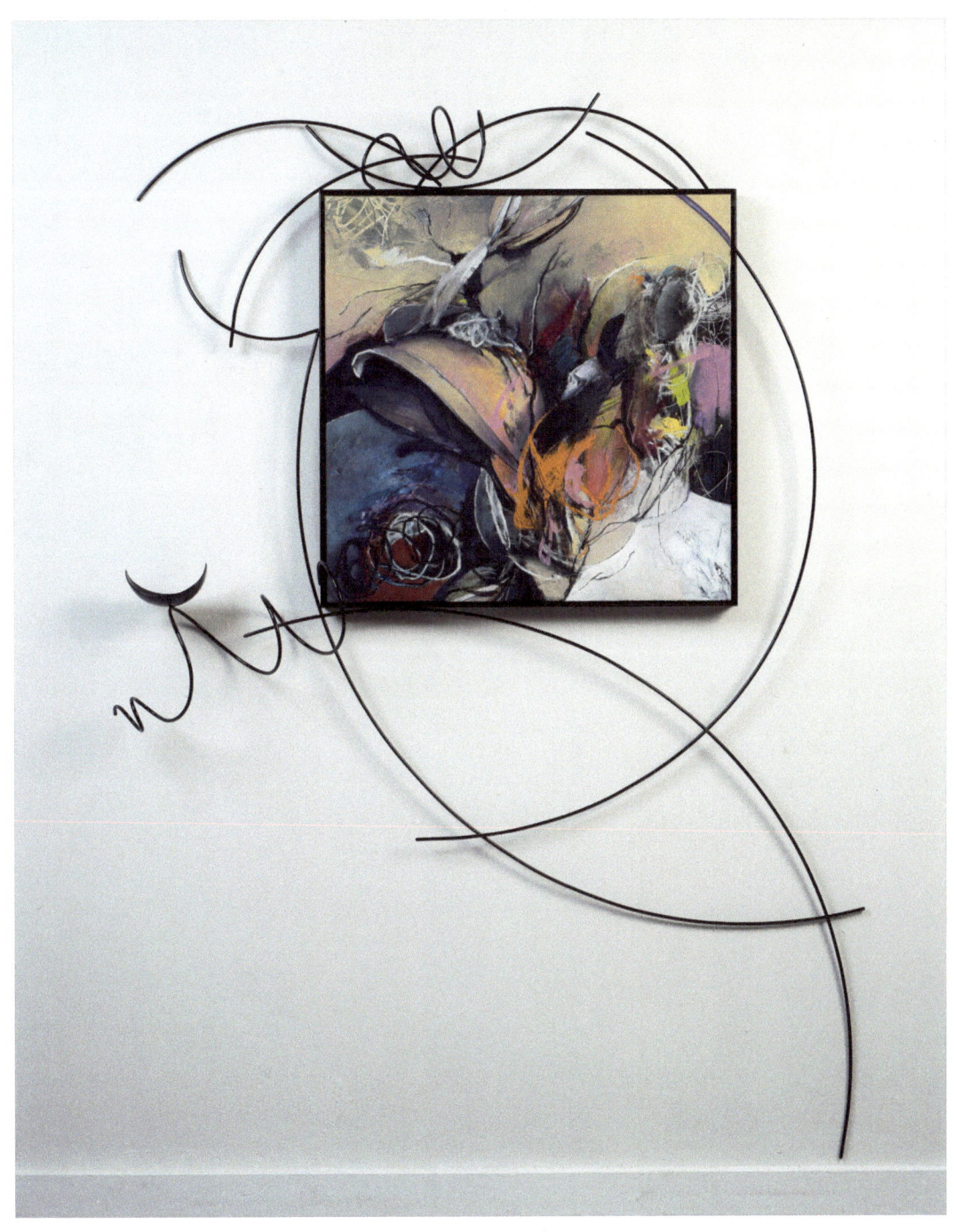

Kim Thoman, *Entanglement 6*, 2017, Oil and steel wall hanging, 72x58x10 in.

Sandy Walker, *Stehekin Summer 14 #9*, 2014, Oil pastel on paper, 22x30 in.

Sandy Walker, *Figures 1*, 2012, Woodblock print, 50x38 in.

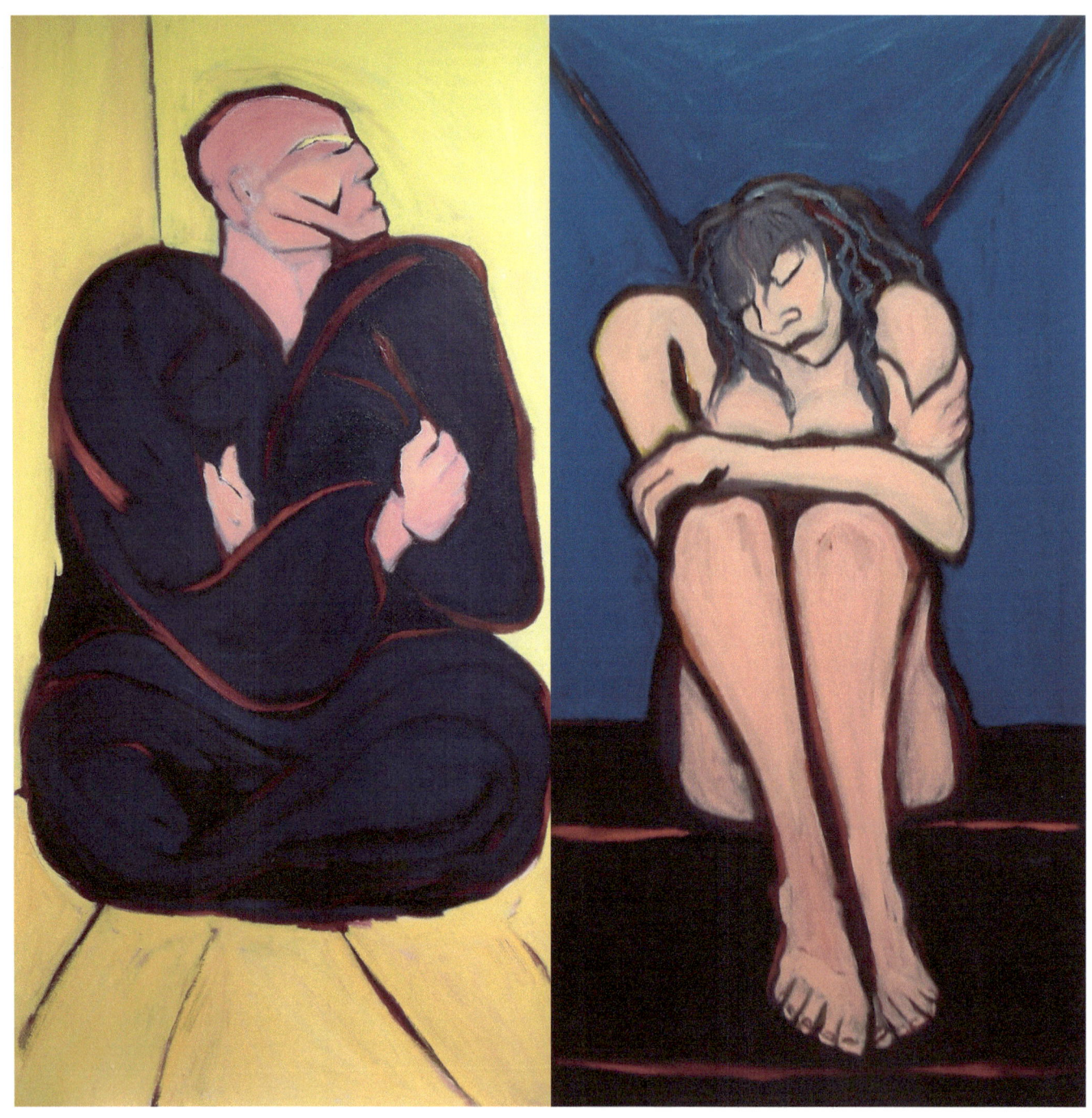

Jan Wurn, *Meditation,* 2012, Oil on canvas, diptich, 48x48 in.

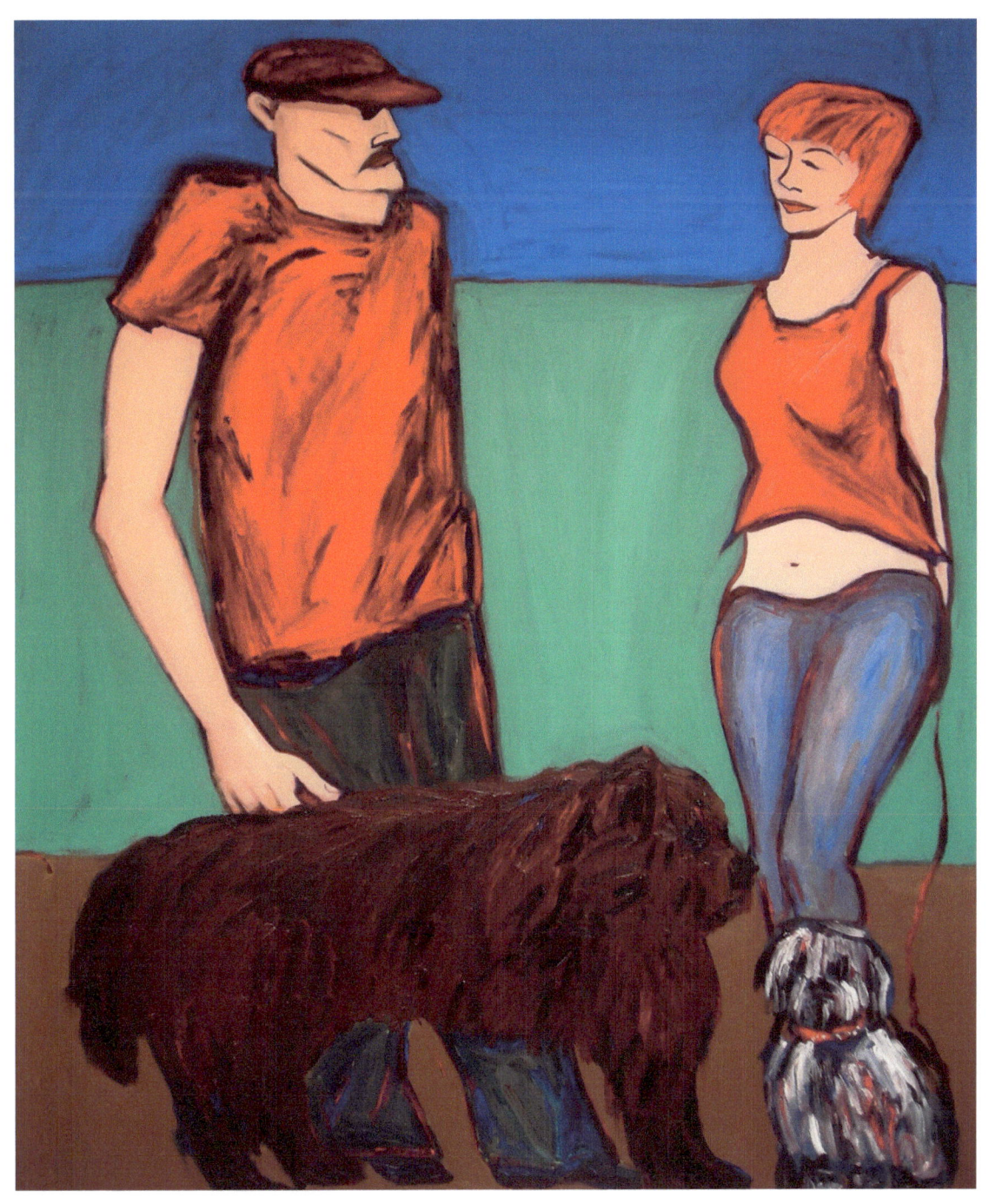

Jan Wurm, *Dog Walk,* n.d., Oil on canvas, 60x48 in.

The Breakfast Group Virtually in Alameda

K Gallery
at Rhythmix Cultural Works

September 12-October 30, 2020

Donna Fenstermaker
John Friedman
Nancy Genn
Katie Hawkinson
Stan Huncilman
Carol Ladewig
Loren Rehbock
Foad Satterfield
Robert Simons
Joseph Slusky
Kim Thoman
Sandy Walker
Jan Wurm

K Gallery
The K Gallery at Rhythmix Cultural Works
supports RCW's mission to bring people together and build community by inspiring engagement in the arts. Exhibitions in the K Gallery reflect the vitality of local artists in the Bay Area community. K Gallery was chosen BEST art gallery in Alameda, by an Alameda Magazine ballot in 2016.

K Gallery presents six visual art exhibitions annually and a weekly Art Jam, where local artists create in a shared studio environment. (pre-covid19)

K Gallery is named for Kazuko (Kay) Koike, one of Rhythmix's founding donors.
"Kazu" is the Japanese word for "peace," "ko" means "child."
Kazuko Koike, child of peace 1919-2020.

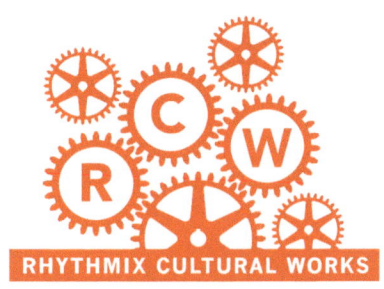

www.ingramcontent.com/pod-product-compliance
Lightning Source LLC
Chambersburg PA
CBHW042029230526
45474CB00006B/54